Thomas

Also by EKO

THE UNSEALED ARCHIVES

King David: Gangster Tragedy

Judas: The Expendable Asset

George: The Unseen War

Kennedy: Shadow Clearance

Jackson: Blood Veto

Unabomber: Control Subject

Patton: Iron Testament

Nixon: Sealed Testimony

McCarthy: Guilty Knowledge

THE KINGDOM WITHIN

The Jesus Frequency

Parables Unsealed

After Jesus

THE NAZARENE

Son of Man

Thomas

Dead Letter

The Unsealed Archives
Book 16

EKO

978-1-971695-20-4

This is a work of creative interpretation. It draws from historical sources but reimagines events and motivations for narrative purposes.

First Edition: July 2026

ekolovesyou.com

A Job worth doing
is worth doing right

— Myers Anderson

Chapter 1

The Kitchen

The radio was talking about a storm coming up out of the Caribbean.

It sat on top of the icebox, a brown plastic Philco with a cracked dial, running on a battery because the power had been out since Monday. A man's voice read wind speeds and compass bearings.

Clarence sat at the kitchen table. His brother Myers sat beside him. The table was pine, scrubbed soft. A kerosene lamp stood between them in the center. The flame was low. The chimney glass was clean. Their great-aunt had cleaned it that afternoon before she lit it.

She stood now at the wood stove, her back to them, turning hominy in a skillet with a wooden spoon. The hominy smelled of lard and pepper and corn. Outside the window the sky had gone the color of lead where the sun had been.

A truck pulled into the yard.

The engine cut. A door opened. Boots on dirt. The screen door at the front of the house creaked and shut. A man crossed the front room into the kitchen behind them. Clarence did not turn. He knew the floorboards.

"Evening, son."

"Evening, Aunt."

Hands came down on the back of Clarence's chair. Big hands. The knuckles scarred where the oil line couplings had bitten them. A thumb rested on the wood an inch from his shoulder.

"Radio's calling it a hurricane."

"It is."

"How long's the power been out?"

"Since Monday."

The hands lifted off the chair. Boots crossed the kitchen. A stool creaked under weight. The oil-company overalls settled. Clarence could see the suspenders from the corner of his eye, denim-blue where they came over the shoulder and crossed the back of the chair. He could see the hands come together on the table, folded.

He did not look up.

The great-aunt brought two tin plates to the table. Hominy. A piece of fatback. A slice of bread. She set one in front of Clarence and one in front of Myers. She did not set one in front of the man.

"I've et."

"You ain't."

"I've et."

She went back to the stove.

Clarence picked up his fork. He did not eat yet. Myers looked at him. Myers was five. Myers was waiting.

The man's hands turned on the table. The left hand opened. A pale line crossed the palm where the couplings had cut him twenty years before.

"Eat."

Clarence ate. Myers ate.

The radio said the storm would be at the Georgia coast by dawn.

The man spoke to the table.

"I'm taking them up to Savannah in the morning."

The great-aunt turned. She held the wooden spoon in her hand and did not wipe it on her apron. She said nothing.

"Can't manage them down here no more. Your sister can't neither. Not with this weather."

"I know it."

"Got the room fixed up. Got a bed apiece."

A silence.

"It's settled."

She turned back to the stove. The spoon moved again.

The man's hands were still folded on the table. Clarence watched them. His fork rested in his hand.

"Boy."

Clarence did not look up.

"Clarence."

He looked up.

He did not see the face. The kerosene lamp threw the light upward, onto the ceiling, onto the great-aunt at the stove, onto the brown Philco on the icebox. The man across the table was a silhouette. A suspender. A shoulder. A jaw in shadow. The hands on the table.

"You hear me?"

"Yes, sir."

"We ain't got no education. Me and your grandmother. We ain't got no chance at what's out there. You all are going to have a chance. You understand me?"

"Yes, sir."

"You'll have it because I'll see that you have it. You will not waste it. You will not lay it down. If I see you lay it down I will take it from you and give it to somebody who won't. You understand, boy?"

"Yes, sir."

"Eat."

Clarence ate.

The radio said the storm was a hundred and ten miles out and coming at thirteen knots. The great-aunt turned down the flame on the kerosene lamp with two fingers, wetting them first on her tongue. The room darkened. The hands on the table stayed folded. Myers put down his fork and watched his brother. Clarence put down his fork and watched the man he could not see.

In the morning the oil truck took them up the coast to the house on East Thirty-Second Street.

The radio was still on when they left.

Chapter 2

The Row

The field was forty acres of dirt held together by pine stumps and memory.

The grandfather had bought it in 1957 off a white farmer in Liberty County who thought the soil was done and sold it for less than the price of the fence around it. The grandfather had walked the boundary with a notebook and taken a handful of the red clay and rolled it between his palms and said nothing and written a check.

Now it was dawn. October 1958.

Clarence stood at the edge of the eastern section in a pair of overalls that had been his brother's two summers before. His boots were his own. A water jug with a wire bail hung from his left hand. The jug was tin and the water was cold and the wire had already cut into the soft meat between his thumb and forefinger.

The tractor was a Massey-Harris 101. Green-painted once. Rust-painted now. The grandfather had paid a hundred and forty dollars for it and kept it running for three years on parts he forged himself in the shed behind the Savannah house.

The grandfather stood beside it.

He wore the same denim overalls he wore on the oil truck, and the same suspenders, and the same boots. The sun had not yet risen enough to put a shadow on his face. Clarence did not look for one.

"You ever run this alone?"

"No, sir."

"You ever watched me run it."

"Yes, sir. Every summer."

"Then you know it."

The grandfather's hand came up. The palm with the old line across it. He pointed.

"You see the stob."

A wooden stake was driven into the ground three hundred yards to the east. A strip of red cloth had been tied to the top of it and hung limp in the still air.

"Yes, sir."

"You see the other one."

Past the first stake, at the farthest edge of the section, a second stake. Another red strip. Three hundred yards beyond the first.

"Yes, sir."

"Your row runs between them. You set your eye on the far one. You do not set your eye on the near one. The near one will make you snake. The far one will make you true."

"Yes, sir."

"When you come back, the furrow better run as clean as if a surveyor laid it. A job worth doing is worth doing right. You skip a step, you cause problems."

"Yes, sir."

The grandfather did not say anything else. He turned and walked to the fence line and sat down on a stump. He pulled a pouch from the bib of his overalls and filled a pipe.

Clarence put the water jug down in the grass at the edge of the field.

He climbed onto the tractor.

The seat was a sprung iron bowl worn smooth by two summers of the grandfather's back. His boots did not quite reach the pedals, which was why the grandfather had welded blocks onto the clutch and the brake the week before. The blocks were raw steel. They had not been painted yet. His left boot fit the block with a half-inch to spare. He pressed it down and the clutch sank.

He checked the throttle. The choke. The gear. The grandfather had told him the starting sequence eleven times and had made him recite it back three. He recited it now in his head.

He turned the key.

The engine coughed and caught.

He let it warm. He watched the smoke come up out of the stack, blue first, then gray, then white. He waited until the white went clean. The grandfather had told him to wait until the smoke went clean. He waited.

He pushed the clutch. He eased the shifter into first. He gave it throttle. He let the clutch out.

The tractor moved.

He set his eye on the far stake.

The near stake passed under his left front wheel and he did not look at it. He kept his eye on the far one. The red cloth at the top of the far stake was a small rag in the white light of sunrise. He held it in his vision the way he had been told to hold it. He did not blink unless he had to.

The plow behind him cut the ground.

He could not see the furrow from the seat. He could only feel the drag. The drag changed with the depth and he corrected the depth with the hydraulic lever. He corrected the lever by feel because the grandfather had said that a man who watches the plow is a man who is going to crook the row. So he did not watch the plow. He watched the stake.

A crow crossed the sky to his right and he did not watch the crow.

Halfway down the row the drag lightened. He felt it through the seat, a softness under his back. A root. A stump hole. The plow was lifting. He adjusted the lever a quarter-inch down and the drag came back.

The sun came up over the pines to his left. His shadow and the tractor's shadow lay down on the dirt to his right and kept pace with him and did not crook.

Sweat ran into his left eye. He did not wipe it. He let it burn and held the stake.

The field ended. The far stake came up to his left front wheel and he let it pass and he slowed the tractor and he turned it in a wide arc the grandfather had taught him to make. He stopped. He looked back.

The furrow ran behind him.

He did not let himself look at the whole row yet. He let himself look at the last twenty yards. The last twenty yards were straight.

He breathed once.

Then he looked at the whole row.

It ran from the stake behind him to a point on the horizon where the grandfather was walking. The grandfather was walking in the furrow. He had come off the stump. He walked slowly. He did not look up. He looked down at the ground where the plow had cut.

Clarence watched him walk.

The grandfather walked the entire three hundred yards. He stopped twice. At the first stop he squatted and put his hand flat on the cut and lifted the clay and smelled it and put it back. At the second stop he nudged a clod with the side of his boot and moved on.

At the end of the row, at the stake where the tractor stood, the grandfather stopped. He took the pipe out of his mouth. He looked at the furrow one more time. He looked at the boy.

He nodded once.

He did not say anything.

He turned and walked back to the stump.

Clarence put the tractor in gear. He let the clutch out. He turned the wheel. He set his eye on the far stake on the second row and he cut the second furrow of his life into the red ground in Liberty County, Georgia.

Chapter 3

The Seminary

Conception, Missouri, sat in the northwestern corner of the state where the land rolled and the sky was bigger than it should have been. The seminary had been built by Benedictines in 1873 out of brick the color of dried blood. Inside the brick was a basilica. Outside the brick was a prairie. Between them, for a hundred years, the priests had kept house.

In April 1968 Clarence Thomas was nineteen years old and had been at the seminary since the previous September.

He was the only Black man in his class.

He was the only Black man in the building.

The grandfather had asked him once, before he left Savannah, whether he understood what he was walking into. Clarence had said yes, sir. The grandfather had said *we'll see.* That was the last thing the grandfather had said to him about the seminary.

That evening after dinner the men of the first-year class gathered in the common room on the second floor of the dormitory wing. A radio sat on a side table near the window. Someone had turned it on for the weather because a storm was supposed to come up from the Ozarks. The radio was tuned to KFEQ out of St. Joseph and instead of weather it was playing bulletins.

Memphis.

Motel.

A shot from across the street.

The room got quiet. No one moved.

Clarence stood by the radiator. His hands were at his sides. His breviary was open in his left hand. He had been reading the Office when the bulletin started and he had not closed the book.

The announcer said that Dr. King had been taken to St. Joseph's Hospital in critical condition.

The announcer came back ten minutes later.

The announcer said that Dr. King had been pronounced dead at 7:05 p.m. Central Standard Time.

Nobody in the common room spoke.

Clarence closed the breviary with his thumb marking the page. He felt the leather binding warm where his hand had been holding it.

A man came down the corridor from the stairs. Clarence knew him by the sound of his walk. He was tall and his heels struck the wood hard. He wore a cassock that was too short for him and showed his ankles.

The man came to the door of the common room. He did not come in. He stood in the doorway and he looked at the radio and then he looked at the men in the room and he said one word and one sentence.

"Good."

There was a pause.

"I hope he dies."

The radio had already said that he had died.

Nobody in the room spoke.

Clarence did not look at the man. He looked at the floor. The floor was pine and had been waxed that morning. His reflection was in the wax where the light from the sconce caught it. He looked at his reflection and he did not move.

The man moved on down the corridor. His heels struck the wood. A door opened and shut.

The radiator ticked.

Someone cleared his throat.

The men in the room spoke, slowly, about the weather.

Clarence walked out of the common room. He walked down the corridor in the other direction. He walked to the stairs. He walked up the stairs to the third floor.

He stopped on the third-floor landing.

He did not know why he stopped. He stopped.

The landing had a window that looked east over the prairie. The sun had set and the prairie was black and the sky above it was blue going to purple going to black. A single light showed where a farmhouse was. The farmhouse was seven miles away and belonged to a man whose name he did not know.

He stood on the landing and looked at the light.

He could hear himself breathe.

He thought of his grandfather. His palm went to the windowpane. He held it there.

He turned and walked down the corridor to his room.

His room was the fourth door on the right. It had a bed and a desk and a chair and a crucifix and a washstand. The crucifix was above the bed. The washstand was under the window. The window looked out on the same prairie as the landing window, only lower.

He took his suitcase from under the bed.

The suitcase was brown cardboard and had belonged to his mother. The handle was wrapped in electrical tape. The tape had gone soft in places.

He opened the suitcase on the bed.

He took his shirts and his pants from the wardrobe and folded them into the suitcase. He took his socks and his undershirts from the dresser and put them on top. He took the rosary from the nail by the bed and he looked at it for a second and then he wound it around his hand and put it in his pocket.

He took the picture of his grandmother off the desk. He took the picture of his brother. He put both pictures face-down on top of the clothes.

He did not take the breviary.

He did not take the crucifix.

He shut the suitcase.

He latched it.

He sat on the edge of the bed.

He looked at his hands. His hands were trembling the way they trembled when he had too much coffee. He watched them tremble and he watched them stop.

The radiator in the room ticked.

Outside the window the prairie went on being dark.

He stood up. He lifted the suitcase by the taped handle. He walked to the door. He opened the door. He looked down the corridor.

The corridor was empty.

He went to the end of the corridor. He passed the common room. The radio was still on. The men in the room were no longer speaking about the weather. He did not look in.

He walked out of the dormitory through the side door that opened on the chapel garden.

It was cold. His breath showed.

He walked down the gravel path to the road. At the road he stopped. He turned once and looked at the seminary. The brick in the moonlight was the color of old rust. A light burned in a window on the second floor where the common room was.

He turned and walked south.

He did not come back.

Chapter 4

The Chapel

The bus from Boston to Worcester ran at dawn for the kids who had gotten themselves into something they did not want to bring home.

Clarence rode the dawn bus.

He sat in the fourth row from the back. He had the aisle. A white boy in an army jacket slept across the double seat next to him and did not wake when the bus took the curves on 290 west. The driver had the radio on low. The radio was playing a woman singing a ballad he did not recognize.

His jacket was army-green. He had bought it in a surplus store on Mass Ave the summer before. The pocket over his left breast held a book. The book was *The Wretched of the Earth.* He had underlined eighty pages of it in red pen. The pen was in the pocket next to the book. The pen had leaked. His shirt under the jacket was stained.

His right hand was wrapped in a blue bandana. The bandana had been clean the previous afternoon. It was not clean now. Under the bandana the knuckles on two fingers had split.

The march had started at Harvard Yard.

He could not remember whose idea it had been to go to Cambridge. He had gotten on a bus with six men he knew from the Black Student Union. The bus had reached Cambridge by two in the afternoon. The march had started at four. By dark it was not a march.

A cop had swung a baton at a kid in front of him and Clarence had gone forward and put his own body between the baton and the kid and the cop had not swung again. Somebody behind him had thrown a brick through the window of a bank. The glass had come down on the street in a long sheet. A boy he did not know had put a fist through the side of a parked car and Clarence had gone forward and put his own fist through the glass of the driver-side window. He did not stop. He did not know how.

The glass had split two knuckles.

He did not know what had happened to the kid with the baton.

He watched the sun come up over Framingham and then over Westborough and then over Shrewsbury. The light came in through the right-hand windows of the bus. The woman on the radio finished her song and a man came on and talked about the weather.

The bus reached Worcester at 4:47 a.m.

He got off at the corner of Main and Pleasant and walked south. His boots made more sound on the pavement than he wanted them to. The city was empty. The streetlights were still on. The air had the cold smell of early April in New England, damp and mineral, the smell of the ground thawing.

He walked up College Hill.

At the top of the hill the campus lay out before him in the grey light. The dormitories. Fenwick Hall. The library. The gravel drive curved around the quad and the grass was coming back after the winter.

On his left, set back from the drive, was the chapel.

St. Joseph Memorial Chapel stood on a small rise. Stone. A low steeple. The doors at the top of a short flight of granite steps. A lamp above the doors burned through the night and was still burning now.

He stopped at the foot of the steps.

He had walked past this chapel every morning for nineteen months and had not gone in once. He had passed it on his way to class, on his way to the meetings of the Black Student Union, on his way to the bus he had ridden down to Cambridge the previous afternoon. He had not looked at the doors.

He looked at the doors now.

The doors did not open. He did not open them.

His right hand came up to the stone railing of the steps. The stone was colder than the air. He pressed his palm flat against it. He felt the cold come into the heel of his hand and up into the wrist.

He said something.

He said it under his breath. He said it once. He said it to nobody he could see.

Lord, take hate out of my heart.

The words went nowhere. No one heard them. The lamp above the doors of the chapel burned. A crow called from the tree line behind Fenwick Hall. The sun came up a little further over Worcester.

He took his hand off the railing.

He did not go into the chapel.

He walked past it. He walked across the quad. He walked to his dormitory and up the stairs to his room on the third floor.

His roommate was asleep. The room smelled of unwashed laundry and pipe tobacco. Clarence did not turn on the light.

He sat down on the edge of his bed in his jacket and his boots.

He took the book out of his pocket. He looked at the cover. He put the book back in the pocket.

He unwrapped the bandana from his right hand and looked at the split knuckles. Dried blood on the cloth. Dried blood on the two fingers. He re-wrapped the hand and let it rest on his thigh.

He sat on the edge of the bed and did not move.

Outside the window, the sun came up.

Chapter 5

The Long Road Out

The letter came in November of 1971. It was addressed in the grandfather's hand. Thick pencil, leaning right, each letter gone over twice where the lead had gotten dull.

Clarence was at Yale.

He took the letter out of the mailbox in the vestibule of 87 Wall Street and looked at it and did not open it. He walked up the stairs to his room. He set it on the desk next to a stack of casebooks. He placed a coffee cup on it to weight it down. The coffee in the cup was from that morning and had gone cold.

He studied torts until two in the morning and went to bed and did not open the letter.

The letter was still on the desk in January. It was

still on the desk in May when he packed the desk into the trunk of a borrowed Pinto and drove west.

* * *

The assistant attorney general's office in Jefferson City was on the third floor of the old Supreme Court building. The ceilings were fourteen feet high. The windows looked south over the capitol lawn. Clarence had a desk and a chair and a bookcase and a brass lamp that had belonged to a judge who had died in 1948.

He put the letter in the bottom drawer of the desk.

John Danforth came into his office one afternoon in the spring of 1975 and sat on the corner of the desk and asked him what he was working on. Clarence said *Missouri v. Hagan.* Danforth said *that the assault case.* Clarence said *yes sir.* Danforth looked at him for a long second and said *you know the thing I like about you, Clarence.* Clarence waited. Danforth said *you don't talk unless there's something to say.* He got off the desk. He left.

The letter stayed in the drawer.

* * *

Monsanto wore a blue tie and a white shirt and a gray suit.

The office was in Creve Coeur and had a view of a parking lot. The lawyers called each other by their last names.

He did agricultural chemical litigation for two years. He did not tell anyone where he had gone to law school. He did not tell anyone where he was from. He came in at seven and went home at eight.

* * *

Danforth went to the Senate in 1977. He called Clarence in the fall of 1979 and said come to Washington.

He went.

The apartment in Washington was a studio on East Capitol Street. The window looked across the street at a row house with a blue door. He did not know who lived behind the blue door. He saw a woman go in and out of it twice a day and never learned her name.

The letter came with him, in a cardboard box with his two diplomas and the photograph of his grandmother.

It went on the top shelf of the closet behind a

duffel bag of winter clothes he had not unpacked since New Haven.

He drafted legislation for Danforth for eighteen months. None of it carried his name.

* * *

One night in January of 1981 he came home to the studio and sat at the kitchenette and ate a sandwich and did not turn on the television. The phone rang. A man said his name. The man said the incoming administration was looking at him for assistant secretary for civil rights at the Department of Education.

Clarence said he would think about it.

He hung up the phone.

He stood in the kitchenette and looked at the blue door across the street through the window above the sink. The woman came out of the blue door at 10:14 p.m., as she did every week, and walked south down East Capitol toward the Library of Congress.

He walked to the closet.

He took the box down from the top shelf.

He set the box on the bed.

He opened the flaps of the box.

He looked at the letter.

He looked at it for a full minute. The envelope

was thin and the paper inside showed through where the light caught it. The grandfather's handwriting on the front had faded a little in the decade since New Haven. The ink of the postmark had faded more.

He closed the flaps of the box.

He put the box back on the top shelf of the closet.

In the morning he called the man back and said yes.

The letter stayed in the box.

Chapter 6

The Agency

The EEOC occupied the ninth and tenth floors of a building on L Street. The carpet was gray. The walls were beige. The ceiling was acoustical tile with water stains where the pipes above had leaked.

Clarence Thomas became chairman on May 6, 1982.

The first morning he walked into the chairman's office he found a stack of pending cases three feet high on the desk. He sat down and lifted the top folder off the stack and opened it.

The folder held the case of a Black woman in Tupelo who had been passed over for a promotion at the sewing plant where she had worked for eleven years. The white woman who got the promotion had worked there for two.

He read the file for forty minutes.

He picked up the phone.

* * *

The call came on the morning of March 30, 1983.

He picked up the phone. His sister Emma Mae said *he is gone.*

He did not ask who.

He told his secretary to book a flight to Savannah and he closed the folder he had been reading and stood up and put on his coat.

The plane came in low over the marsh that night. He saw the water and the grass and the oyster beds and the single lights of the houses along the Intracoastal. He could not tell which of the lights was the grandfather's.

The funeral was held at St. Benedict the Moor. The pews were oak. The pallbearers were five men he did not know and one man he did. The casket was pine. It had been built by a carpenter in Liberty County who had known the grandfather for forty years and who did not charge the grandmother for the wood.

After the service he drove alone to the house on East Thirty-Second Street.

He let himself in with the key the grandmother had given him in 1968. She was staying at his aunt's that night. The house was empty.

The kitchen had the same linoleum. A newer radio sat on the shelf above the icebox where the Philco had been. The shelf was pine and had been sanded smooth by the grandmother's hand.

He stood at the table.

He took his coat off and hung it on the back of a chair.

From the inside breast pocket of the coat he took an envelope.

He had carried it for eleven years and four months.

He sat at the table.

The envelope was thin. The paper inside showed through where the light caught it. The grandfather's handwriting on the front had faded. The ink of the postmark was almost gone.

He turned the envelope over.

He slit it with his thumbnail.

He removed the single sheet folded inside.

He unfolded it.

He read it.

He read it again.

He folded it.

He put it back in the envelope.

He put the envelope back in the inside pocket of his coat.

He sat at the table for a long time. The clock on the wall above the wood stove ticked. Outside, a car passed on East Thirty-Second Street.

He stood up. He put on his coat. He left the house and locked the door with the key the grandmother had given him in 1968.

In the morning he flew back to Washington.

* * *

The following week the Washington Post ran an op-ed calling him a sellout.

He read it in his office before the staff came in. He read it twice. He put the newspaper in the trash can under his desk.

The woman in Tupelo got her promotion in June of 1984. Clarence called her from his office and told her and she said *I knew the Lord would make a way* and he said *yes ma'am* and hung up the phone and did not tell anyone he had called her.

The NAACP condemned him twice that same year.

He did not respond.

* * *

He met Virginia Lamp at a conference in New York in the summer of 1986. She was blonde, from Nebraska. She laughed at a joke he made about the fire escape outside the window of the hotel ballroom. He married her in May of 1987 in Omaha. Her father said the benediction.

* * *

The stack on his desk never got below two feet.

Every morning he started at the top and read until lunch. Every afternoon he started at the top and read until six. At six he went home to the apartment in Virginia and ate dinner with his wife and talked about her day and did not talk about his own.

He stayed eight years.

In the summer of 1989 the phone on his desk rang.

A man from the White House said the president

was considering him for the Court of Appeals for the District of Columbia Circuit.

Clarence said he would think about it.

He hung up the phone.

He looked at the stack of folders on his desk. Two feet two inches high. It had been two feet two inches high the morning he walked in. The folders changed. The stack did not.

He picked up the phone and called the man from the White House back.

He accepted the nomination.

He hung up the phone. He lifted the top folder off the stack. He opened it. He read.

Chapter 7

The Bench

The Senate confirmed him by voice vote in March of 1990. No one objected.

He took the oath on the twelfth of March in the east courtroom of the E. Barrett Prettyman Courthouse at Constitution and John Marshall Place. His wife held the Bible. He put his left hand on it. He raised his right hand. He said the words.

The clerk handed him the robe.

* * *

The robe was heavier than he had expected.

It was black and it was long and it was made of a

wool so dense the lining had to be quilted or it would not hang. He put it on in the chambers on the sixth floor that the previous judge had left three weeks before. The chambers smelled of pipe smoke and leather and the paper of old briefs. A window looked out onto a brick courtyard where a sycamore was in first bud.

His reflection was in the glass of a framed lithograph on the wall. He did not look at it.

He walked down the hall to the bench.

* * *

Judge Laurence Silberman had the chambers three doors down. He was sixty-four. He had been ambassador to Yugoslavia in the middle of the seventies and had come back and not spoken about it. He wore a bow tie every day.

He found Clarence in the law library on a Thursday afternoon in April.

Clarence had a case on the bench Monday. He had been reading it for six hours. The case concerned an agricultural labor dispute in Virginia involving a migrant crew and a contract the crew foreman could not read.

Silberman pulled out the chair across the table and sat down.

"You're going to be on the Court in two years."

Clarence looked up.

"Sir?"

"I said what I said."

"The Supreme Court."

"Yes."

"I have been on this court for thirty-one days."

"I know that."

Silberman folded his hands on the table. The hands were old and there were liver spots on the backs.

"I want you to listen to me, Clarence."

"Yes, sir."

"There is one question you need to answer before that call comes. The call is going to come. It will come on an ordinary day. You will have five minutes. You will not have time to think about anything you have not already thought about."

"Yes, sir."

"The question is this."

Silberman leaned back in the chair.

"What are you afraid of."

Clarence did not answer.

“I’ll leave you to it.”

Silberman stood up. He pushed the chair in. He walked out of the library.

Clarence sat at the table with the legal pad in front of him. He set down his pen. He looked at the pad. He looked at his hand.

He wrote nothing.

* * *

The call came on a Sunday at the end of June of 1991.

He was on the deck of his brother-in-law’s house on the Chesapeake with a fishing reel in his lap. His wife handed him the cordless phone. She did not say who it was. He took the phone. He put it to his ear.

A voice said *the President would like to see you.*

Clarence stood up. He set the reel down on the deck. He walked to the end of the dock and looked at the water. The water was gray. A gull crossed from the Eastern Shore to the Western Shore and did not stop.

He said *yes sir.*

He hung up.

He walked back to the house and told his wife.

She said *what did you tell him.*

He said *I told him yes.*

She said *are you ready.*

He watched the boats on the Bay. He looked at his wife.

"No," he said.

"Who would be," she said.

Chapter 8

The Nomination

They flew to Kennebunkport on the morning of the first of July in a military plane out of Andrews. The President's people sat in the front of the cabin. Clarence and Virginia sat in the back. The flight was an hour and forty minutes.

Outside the window the coast of Maine came into view. Granite and spruce and the cold blue Atlantic. A fishing boat out on the water. Rockweed on the shore.

The car that met them on the tarmac was a black Lincoln. The driver did not speak. The drive to Walker's Point was thirty-five minutes.

* * *

The house sat on the point. Gray shingle. White trim. A low picket fence along the seaward side where the rocks went down to the water. A staff had set up a lectern on the lawn. A rope line kept the press twenty yards back. The sky was clear. A wind off the water moved the bunting on the lectern.

The President came out of the house in a blue blazer and a red tie. Barbara was with him. Two Secret Service men came behind them.

The President shook Clarence's hand. He said *I'm glad you're here.* Clarence said *yes sir.*

They stood on the lawn and waited for the press to settle.

The President stepped to the lectern.

He said this was the best person for the job.

He said his name.

* * *

Clarence took the lectern.

He had a page of notes in his coat pocket. He did not take it out.

He looked past the press, at the sea.

He said he had come a long way from where he had started.

He said a sharecropper's grandson from Pin Point, Georgia.

He said my grandparents, Myers and Christine Anderson, raised me. He said they were the strongest.

He stopped.

He did not continue the sentence.

He looked down at the lectern. He wiped his left eye with the back of his left hand. He looked up.

He said only in America could this have been possible.

He said he thanked God for the men and women who had come before him.

The wind off the water moved his tie. A Secret Service man in a dark suit looked at the ground.

He finished speaking.

He stepped back from the lectern.

The President came up beside him and put a hand on his shoulder.

Clarence did not look at him.

He was looking at a boat out on the water. A small white boat with a single sail. The sail was up but slack. The boat was not moving. There was no one on the deck that he could see.

* * *

On the flight back to Washington Virginia held his hand.

The plane lifted off the runway at Brunswick and climbed through a layer of cloud and came out above it. The sun was behind them now. The light on the top of the cloud was pink going to gold.

He did not speak.

She did not either.

After a while she said *they'll come at you.*

He said *I know it.*

She said *are you afraid.*

He said nothing. She did not press him.

At the descent into Andrews he said *yes.*

* * *

That night in the house in Virginia he could not sleep.

He got out of bed at two in the morning and went to the kitchen and did not turn on the light. He stood at the window above the sink and looked at the yard. A neighbor's motion light was on at the fence line. A raccoon crossed the grass, worked the lid off a trash can, and went over the fence with something in its mouth.

He stood at the window.

From the inside breast pocket of the coat that was hanging on the back of a chair in the kitchen he took an envelope.

The slit he had made in the top with his thumbnail eight years ago was still clean. The flap had never been folded back down. He had been carrying it open.

He held it in his hand.

The motion light at the fence went off.

He put the envelope back in the coat.

He went to bed.

He lay on his back in the dark and looked at the ceiling and waited for morning.

Chapter 9

The Rope

The hearing room was in the Russell Senate Office Building. Caucus Room 325. The ceiling was twenty-eight feet high. The room held a press gallery, a public gallery, and three rows of cameras. The microphone on the witness table was a gooseneck and the tape over the cable on the floor was gaffer's black.

The first round opened on the tenth of September.

He sat at the table for eight hours a day for five days. His wife sat behind him in the second row of the gallery. She wore blue. She did not speak during the testimony. She did not speak during the recesses. She brought him coffee. She brought him a sandwich. When he stood up she stood up. When he sat down she sat down.

The questions were about natural law.

The questions were about abortion.

He answered what he would answer. He did not answer what he would not. The senators leaned into their microphones. The senators leaned back in their chairs. The chairman of the committee, a man from Delaware with a long face, ran the clock.

On Friday the twenty-seventh of September the committee deadlocked seven to seven.

On the first of October the Senate set the floor vote for the eighth.

* * *

On the sixth of October at six in the morning Newsday published a story.

By eight NPR had it.

By noon the nominee's office had the file.

The file contained an affidavit from a Yale-educated Black woman who had worked for him at the EEOC. She said he had harassed her at the agency. She said he had talked about a pubic hair on a can of Coke.

The chairman reopened the hearings.

He flew back to Washington on a Thursday. He got to the house in Virginia at ten in the evening. He sat at the kitchen table in a shirt that was wet at the collar. Virginia sat across from him with her hands folded on the table. The lamp above the table was the only light on in the house.

She said *do you want to withdraw.*

He said *no.*

She said *tell me why.*

He said *because I will not allow them to take what they will take if I do.*

He did not cry.

He did not raise his voice.

He sat at the table and he looked at the grain of the wood.

* * *

The hearing reopened on the eleventh of October. The room was fuller than it had been in September. Every camera in the city was in the room. The cable on the floor had been doubled.

The witness went first. She was calm. She testified for eight hours. Her voice did not shake. She did not look at him and he did not look at her.

He went second.

The chairman called him at five minutes to nine in the evening. He took the oath. He sat at the table. His wife sat behind him in the second row. She was in blue again. She held her handbag in her lap and she did not move.

The chairman asked him a question.

He said the statement was false.

The chairman asked him another question.

He said he had nothing more to say about the specifics.

He said he would not address them again.

He said he had something else he wanted to say.

The chairman nodded.

He leaned toward the microphone.

He said this is a circus.

He said it is a national disgrace.

He said and from my standpoint, as a Black American, as far as I am concerned, it is a high-tech lynching for uppity Blacks who in any way deign to think for themselves, to do for themselves, to have different ideas.

He said you will be lynched, destroyed, caricatured by a committee of the United States Senate rather than hung from a tree.

The chairman did not interrupt.

The room was as quiet as the room had ever been.

He said he was a victim of this process and he was not going to sit there and gratify it.

He stopped.

He did not continue.

He looked at the chairman. He looked at the wood of the table.

* * *

That night he did not go home.

He slept on the couch in his lawyer's office on K Street. He had his coat folded under his head. He did not take off his shoes. The overhead fluorescent in the reception area stayed on all night. The building hummed.

At three in the morning he got up and walked to the bathroom and stood at the sink with his hands on the cold porcelain and looked at his face in the mirror.

His eyes were red. A day's growth of beard. The collar of his shirt was yellow where the sweat had dried.

He looked at himself for a long time.

He said something.

He said it to the man in the mirror. He said it once. He said it under his breath.

Lord, take hate out of my heart.

He turned off the light.

He went back to the couch.

He did not sleep.

* * *

The Senate voted on the fifteenth.

Fifty-two in favor.

Forty-eight against.

Chapter 10

The Swearing

The private oath was administered on the eighteenth of October on the South Lawn at four in the afternoon. Justice White read the oath. Virginia held the Bible. A wind out of the northwest took the leaves off the magnolia by the colonnade. The President stood three paces to his left.

He raised his right hand.

He said the words.

* * *

The public investiture was on the twenty-third.

The courtroom was forty-four feet square and had twenty-four columns of Siena marble. The benches were mahogany. Behind the bench, where the nine seats were arranged in a low crescent, the curtain was red velvet with a gold cord.

He walked in behind the marshal.

He took the second oath.

He took his seat at the far left end of the bench, the chair of the junior justice. He placed his hands on the wood.

The wood was cold.

* * *

That evening they drove home to their house in Virginia.

He drove. She sat in the passenger seat. Neither of them spoke for the first twenty minutes. The traffic on the George Washington Parkway was heavy. The sun went down over the river.

At a stoplight she said *I want you to do something for me.*

He said *yes ma'am.*

She said *when this is done, when you are finished, we are going to buy a motor home and we are going to drive it to every Walmart parking lot in this country.*

He looked at her.

"Every one?"

"Every one."

He did not answer right away. The light changed. He put the car in gear. He drove.

After a mile he said *ok*.

She said *you promise*.

He said *I promise*.

They drove the rest of the way home in silence. When they pulled into the driveway the motion light at the fence came on.

The yard was empty.

Chapter 11

The Silence

His chambers were on the third floor of the Supreme Court building, east wing, third door on the right. The window looked out at the Library of Congress across First Street NE.

He stopped asking questions during oral argument.

He had asked questions in his first year on the bench. By the fifth year he had stopped.

He sat at the far left end of the bench and he listened.

When the clerks asked him why, he said he had read the briefs. He said he did not need to hear his own voice in the room in order to think.

He did not explain it in public.

* * *

He worked with a fountain pen. The nib was medium. He used blue-black ink he bought by the bottle. He wrote on a yellow legal pad with his feet crossed under the desk.

He drafted every opinion in longhand first.

The clerks typed the drafts. He revised the typed drafts with the pen. He passed the revised drafts back to the clerks. The clerks retyped them. He revised them again. A signed opinion went through nine drafts on average and never fewer than four.

He was not fast.

He did not aim to be fast.

* * *

The Kelo case came up in February of 2005.

The question was whether the government could take a woman's house by eminent domain and give it to a private developer for the building of a pharmaceutical research park. The woman's name was Susette Kelo. The neighborhood was called Fort Trumbull. New London, Connecticut.

Oral argument was in February.

He listened.

He did not ask a question.

* * *

The Court ruled five to four in favor of the city in June.

He dissented.

He wrote the dissent in the first week of June at the desk in his chambers. The window was open and the sound of traffic on First Street came in. A clerk had brought him a cup of coffee at nine and the cup was still on the desk at one, a cold quarter-inch of coffee in the bottom.

He wrote in longhand on the yellow pad.

He wrote that something had gone seriously awry with the Court's interpretation of the Constitution.

Citizens were safe from the government in their homes, he wrote, but the homes themselves were not.

The losses would fall disproportionately on poor communities.

He wrote that the Court had erased the Public Use Clause from the Constitution of the United States.

He stopped at the end of the yellow pad. He set the pen down. He looked at what he had written. He picked the pen back up. He crossed out a sentence. He rewrote it. He crossed out another. He rewrote it. He turned the page.

He wrote for three more hours.

At four in the afternoon the clerk came in and asked if he wanted a sandwich. He said no.

At six in the evening he stood up from the desk and put on his coat and walked down the three flights of marble stairs and out the side door.

He sat on a bench in the plaza and looked at the Capitol dome across First Street.

A sewing plant in Tupelo.

A house in Pin Point with no power for four days.

He did not speak.

He stood up. He walked to his car. He drove home.

At home he picked the pen back up.

Chapter 12

The Majority

The Grutter opinion came down in June of 2003. He read it at the desk in his chambers.

Sandra Day O'Connor had written it. The vote was five to four. The University of Michigan Law School could continue to use race as a factor in admissions. She wrote that the racial preferences had to end, that twenty-five years from the date of the opinion should be enough time.

He dissented.

He wrote that racial classifications were unconstitutional.

The Law School had no compelling interest in maintaining a critical mass of Black students.

The admissions program was a naked racial balancing act.

He wrote that a great injustice was being done in his name.

The opinion ran twenty-three pages.

He was fifty-five years old.

* * *

The Dobbs opinion came down in June of 2022, the case that ended the constitutional right to abortion.

He wrote a concurrence. He wrote that substantive due process, the doctrine the Court used to find rights the Constitution never named, was an oxymoron that lacked any basis in the text, and that the Court should reconsider every precedent built on it.

The same week he wrote Bruen. For the Court.

He wrote that the Second Amendment's plain text covered an individual's conduct, that the Constitution presumptively protected that conduct, and that the State had to demonstrate that a firearm regulation was consistent with this Nation's historical tradition.

He did not write a separate concurrence. He was seventy-four years old.

* * *

Students for Fair Admissions was argued on Halloween of 2022.

The oral argument ran for almost five hours. He sat beside the Chief Justice now, one seat from the center, where seniority had carried him as junior justices came in behind him. The mahogany of the new seat was warmer than the mahogany of the old seat.

He asked one question.

He asked the lawyer for Harvard what the endpoint of race-conscious admissions would be.

The lawyer did not give him a straight answer.

He wrote a separate concurrence in the opinion that came down the following June.

He wrote that he was writing separately to offer an originalist defense of the colorblind Constitution.

He wrote that the Fourteenth Amendment meant what it said.

He wrote that the Constitution did not see race and did not allow the government to see race.

The word was not his. More than a century earlier, in a case called Plessy, a justice named Harlan had used it first. Our Constitution is colorblind, he had written, and neither knows nor tolerates classes among citizens.

He had written it in dissent. He had written it alone.

Seven justices held that a State could separate the races by law. Harlan told the seven they were wrong. He was more than forty years in the ground before the Court came to stand where he stood.

Thomas knew the line. He put Harlan in the opinion.

He had written once that he was quite comfortable in the company he kept.

He kept writing.

He wrote that the experiment begun by Grutter had failed.

He wrote that the time was up.

* * *

He was seventy-five the day the opinion came down.

He sat in his chambers after the reading. A clerk had brought him a glass of water. The glass was still on the desk untouched an hour later.

He opened the bottom drawer of his desk.

From the drawer he took a thin envelope. The handwriting on the front was in pencil, leaning right, each letter gone over twice. The slit in the top had been made with a thumbnail forty years before. The flap had never been folded back down.

He removed the single sheet folded inside.

He unfolded it.

He read it.

He read it again.

He folded it.

He put it back in the envelope.

He put the envelope back in the drawer.

He closed the drawer.

He drank the water.

Chapter 13

The Row Redivivus

The motor home came east on US 280 at the end of April of 2026.

He was driving. He had been driving for six days. Virginia had been reading a book in the passenger seat and had gone to sleep at a rest stop outside Columbus and not woken up when he started the engine again.

He crossed into Georgia at eleven in the morning.

The air changed. The color of the dirt at the shoulder of the road changed from the rust of the uplands to the red of the coastal plain.

He took the exit at Ludowici.

* * *

He drove east on Ga-57 through country he had not driven in thirty years.

The towns were smaller than they had been. Some of them were not towns anymore. A store he had stopped at as a boy was a brick shell with the roof fallen in and honeysuckle growing through the front door. A gas station he had stopped at with his brother in 1967 was still there. The pumps were new. The paint on the sign was peeling. The same family had owned it for four generations.

He turned south onto a county road that did not have a number.

The road was paved for the first mile and then it was not.

* * *

The field was at the end of the road.

He stopped the motor home at the fence line. He turned off the engine. He set the parking brake. He got out.

Virginia was awake now. She did not get out with him. She sat in the cab and watched.

He walked through the gate.

* * *

The field was forty acres of dirt held together by pine stumps and memory.

It had been bought by the grandfather in 1957 and farmed by the grandfather until 1979 and leased to a neighbor after that for as long as the neighbor could work it. The neighbor had died some years back. The field had been fallow since.

Clarence walked the field.

He walked it from the eastern fence to the western fence and back. The dirt under his boots was the same red clay it had been in 1958. The pine stumps that had been there in 1958 were there now, gone gray and half-rotted, but still in the ground, holding it together by the roots below.

He walked to the place where the first stake had been.

The stake was gone. The posthole in the ground was filled.

He walked to the place where the second stake had been.

Same.

On the way back he saw a piece of raw steel in the dirt where the plow line had run. He bent and picked it up. One of the welding blocks the grandfather had cut to fit his boots to the pedals. The steel had rusted. The cut edges were still square. He put it in the pocket of his coat.

He stood between the two places where the stakes had been. He looked east toward where the second stake had stood. The morning light fell long across the field in the direction of his shadow.

He stood still for a long time.

He was seventy-seven years old.

* * *

On the way back to the gate he stopped at a low rise in the corner of the field where three live oaks stood together.

The graves were under the oaks.

The grandfather's was on the left. Myers Anderson, 1907 to 1983. The stone was simple granite. Below the name it said *A JOB WORTH DOING*.

The grandmother's was on the right. Christine Anderson, 1911 to 1992. The stone matched. Below her name it said *AND LET WHOSOEVER WILL, COME.*

There was a third stone, smaller, between them. It was for a daughter who had died in infancy in 1942, before Clarence was born.

He stood at the foot of the three stones.

He did not kneel.

He took the envelope out of the inside breast pocket of his coat.

He looked at the envelope one more time.

He bent at the waist and placed it on the ground in front of the grandfather's stone. He weighted it with a small flat piece of granite that lay at the base of the stone and that had not been placed there by any hand he knew.

He stood up.

He walked back to the motor home.

Virginia had not moved from the cab. She watched him come back across the field. When he got to the driver-side door she said nothing. He got in. He closed the door. He sat with his hands on the wheel.

He started the engine.

He backed the motor home out of the gate onto the county road.

He drove.

At the end of the county road he turned onto Ga-57 and drove west.

He did not look back.

He drove.

<3EKO

The Archives are Open

Thank you for reading Thomas.

If this story moved you, consider buying me a coffee.

FUEL THE MISSION

For advance books and the complete archive:

EKOLOVESYOU.COM

About the Author

EKO writes the history they didn't teach you.

The Unsealed Archives treats history as a crime scene. Fingerprints on the money bag, logistics behind the battles, politics behind the miracles. Halos stripped. Humans underneath. When he's not writing, he's in the mountains, riding motorcycles or teaching his kids what the wilderness teaches.

Everything notices. Everything is noticed.

x.com/Ekolovesyou

eko.substack.com

Made in the USA
Monee, IL
16 September 2026

63296734R00049